HEARTS
AND
CRAFTS

Over 20 Projects for Fun-Loving Kids

Jennifer Storey Gillis

Illustrations by Patti Delmonte

A Storey Publishing Book

STOREY

Storey Communications, Inc.

D1441161

8924888

Hearts & Crafts

*The mission of Storey Communications is to serve our customers
by publishing practical information that encourages personal independence
in harmony with the environment.*

Edited by Gwen W. Steege
Cover and text design by Carol J. Jessop and
Wanda Harper Joyce

The information in this book is true and complete
to the best of our knowledge. All recommendations
are made without guarantee on the part of the
author or Storey Communications, Inc. The author
and publisher disclaim any liability in connection
with the use of this information. For additional
information please contact Storey Communications,
Inc., Schoolhouse Road, Pownal, Vermont 05261.

Printed in Canada by Interglobe
Second Printing, November 1995

Library of Congress Cataloging-in-Publication Data

Gillis, Jennifer Storey, 1967–
    Hearts and crafts : over 20 projects for fun-loving
kids / Jennifer Storey Gillis; illustrations by Patti Delmonte.
        p.   cm.
    "A Storey Publishing book."
    Summary: Contains craft projects and recipes with
heart themes, as well as information about a healthy heart.
    ISBN 0-88266-844-7
    1. Handicraft — Juvenile literature. 2. Heart in art
— Juvenile literature.   3. Cookery — Juvenile
literature. 4. Heart — Juvenile literature.
[1. Handicraft. 2. Heart in art. 3. Cookery.
4. Heart.]   I. Delmonte, Patti.   II. Title.
    TT160.G468   1994
    745.5 — dc20   93-4841
                                                 CIP
                                                 AC

Some of the recipes in this book were originally published in
the following Garden Way Publishing publications: page 22
from *Satisfying Soups* by Phyllis Hobson; pages 34–35 from *It's
the Berries!* by Liz Anton and Beth Dooley; pages 36–37 from
Picnic! by Edith Stovel. All titles are available through Storey
Communications, Inc., Schoolhouse Road, Pownal, Vermont
05261 (1-800-827-8673).

Table of Contents

Heart Smart!

Your heart is one of the many parts of your body
that you could not live without. But what do you really
know about it? The first part of this book explains
what your heart is, what it does, and why it so important
to take good care of it. You'll learn how to feed and
exercise your heart, and in return, your heart will
give you many years of loving and living.
Read on to become Heart Smart!

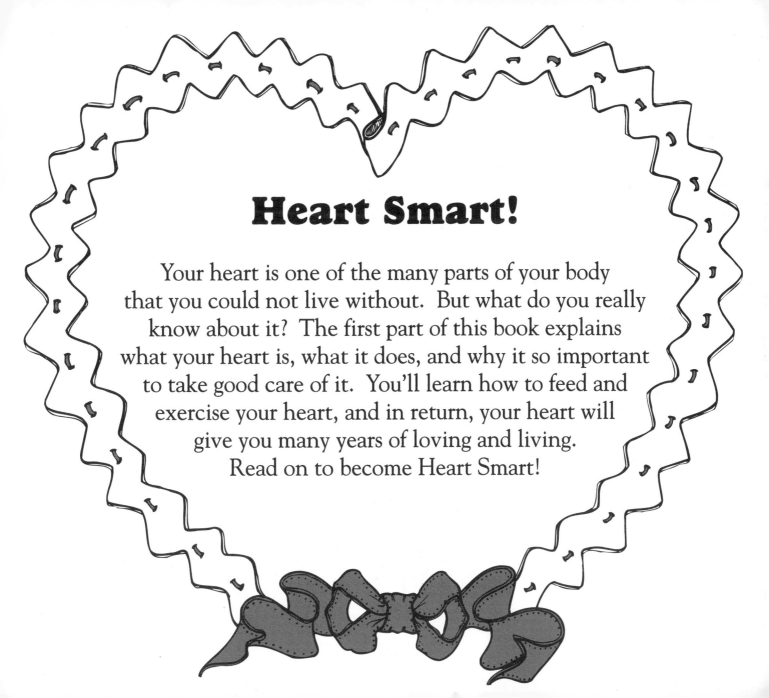

An Interview with Henry Heart

To get an accurate description of what a heart does, let's go straight to the source. The following is an interview with an authority on this subject, Henry Heart!

Mr. Heart, what exactly is your job?

Henry Heart: I work in the Human Body Company, and my official title is Muscular Pump. My job is to move the blood through the body so that all the other offices have enough oxygen and nutrients.

Are you found only in the Human Body?

Henry Heart: No, you can find a heart in all backboned animals, and even in some animals without backbones. Did you know that you can find a relative of mine in an earthworm, in insects, and even in snails?!

Where is your "office" located?

Henry Heart: I am in your chest cavity, a little to the left of the center of your body. I am protected by your rib cage so that I stay safe and sound.

What do you do all day?

Henry Heart: Actually, mine is a 24-hour-a-day job! My left side takes the blood from your lungs and pushes it out through arteries to the rest of your body. Then, my right side takes your blood back from your body through veins and draws it through your lungs. It's easiest to remember this way: *arteries* carry nutrients and oxygen to the body's cells, and *veins* take away the waste from the cells. Did you know that blood coming from the lungs is bright *red* (because it has plenty of oxygen) and blood coming from the rest of your body is *blue* because it needs oxygen?

3

Don't you ever get to rest?

Henry Heart: Sure! I get a half second rest between every beat! I pump, then relax, pump, then relax. When you hear your heart beat, it is me, the pump, pumping blood to your body.

How big are you?

Henry Heart: I am about the size of your two clenched fists. The bigger you are, the bigger I am! Remember, I have lots of work to do.

What is a pulse?

Henry Heart: When you feel your pulse, you can discover how fast I am beating. You can find your pulse anywhere on your body where the blood in an artery is close to the surface. Try to find your pulse by putting your fingers on your throat by your jaw, or on the inside of your wrist. If you are finding someone else's pulse, don't use your thumb, because your thumb has a pulse of its own.

Your heart beats about 100 to 120 times a minute. Small hearts usually beat faster than big ones. A grown-up's heart beats about 60 to 70 times a minute. A mouse's heart beats 700 times a minute and an elephant's only beats 25 times!

Do you understand what high blood pressure is?

Henry Heart: Of course! The harder it is for a heart to pump blood through arteries, the higher the pressure in them becomes. If people damage their arteries by smoking or eating the wrong things, it's hard for the blood to get through. This causes high blood pressure.

Is there anything else that you would like to tell us?

Henry Heart: Well, I don't like to brag but . . . did you know that in 24 hours I can pump enough blood to fill an oil tanker?

Thank you for taking the time out of your busy day to answer our questions, Mr. Heart! Hey, wait a minute — how did you take a break?!

There are miles and miles of blood vessels running through your body!

5

Healthy Heart

Now that you know how your heart keeps you healthy and running,
see what you can do to keep it healthy!

Fortunately, these three things aren't difficult to get!

Good Food

Your heart craves food that is low in fat. Remember what a big job your heart has to do for you. It needs energy to pump your blood all day long, and the best energy does not come from fat! If you eat too much fat, you may make your body *and* your arteries fat. That makes it hard for the blood to get through, and then your heart has to work even harder. Give your heart a break — eat foods that are low in fat! Vegetables, fruit, cereals, pasta, low-fat dairy products, fish, and meats with little or no fat in them are terrific ways to start!

Clean Air

If you remember from our interview with Henry Heart, part of the heart's

After School Snacks

Instead of . . .
Soda
Potato chips
Ice cream

try . . .
Fresh fruit
Pretzels
Frozen yogurt

job is to draw blood through your lungs in order to get oxygen from your lungs and carry it to the rest of your body. If the air you breathe has smoke or pollution in it, then your heart has to pump harder, because it has less oxygen in it! The blood it is getting from the lungs isn't as clean as it

should be, so once again, your heart has to work too hard! The last thing you want is for your heart to quit on you, so make its work environment as pleasant as possible.

Exercise

When you are going to be running in a race or swimming in a swim meet, what do you have to do? Practice! You know you need to work hard to get your legs and arms strong for the race, but did you know that you have to get your heart in shape, too? When you exercise, your pulse speeds up, which means that your heart is beating faster. This helps your heart get in shape, and when your heart is in shape, you feel better, look better, and have more energy. That is why you need to exercise every day. If you didn't ever exercise, soon your heart would be so out of shape that it would have trouble doing its normal job of pumping blood to your body.

Fortunately, it is fun and easy to exercise daily, so your heart should be all set! Here are just twenty of the hundreds of things that you can do to exercise. Try any or all of these to keep your heart in tip-top condition. Can you add more to this list?

- ◆ Baseball
- ◆ Basketball
- ◆ Field hockey
- ◆ Football
- ◆ Frisbee
- ◆ Golf
- ◆ Gymnastics
- ◆ Hockey
- ◆ Hopscotch
- ◆ Ice skating
- ◆ Jumping rope
- ◆ Relay races
- ◆ Running

- ◆ Sledding
- ◆ Skipping
- ◆ Skiing
- ◆ Soccer
- ◆ Swimming
- ◆ Tag
- ◆ Walking

Eat Your Heart Out

You know you should eat good food to keep your heart healthy,
but how do you know what foods are low in fat?

Your classroom or the gymnasium or your doctor's office may have a new chart showing what foods are best for you to eat a lot of, and what foods you should eat only a little of. These foods are arranged in a pyramid, and here is what the pyramid is trying to tell you:

Grains: Grains, including pasta, rice, and breads, give your heart lots of energy, without giving it much fat to worry about.

Fruits and vegetables: You know what these are. Most fruits and vegetables are fat-free, so your heart loves them.

But best of all — they taste great, so fill 'er up!

Dairy products: You need lots of milk and foods made of milk to have healthy bones; strong, white teeth; shiny eyes; and beautiful hair. Milk tastes good and *is* good for you! You should try to stick to low-fat dairy products — skim milk, low-fat yogurt, and low-fat cheese.

Meat or other protein foods: You need a little protein every day to give your body energy, but there are lots of healthful foods to choose from when

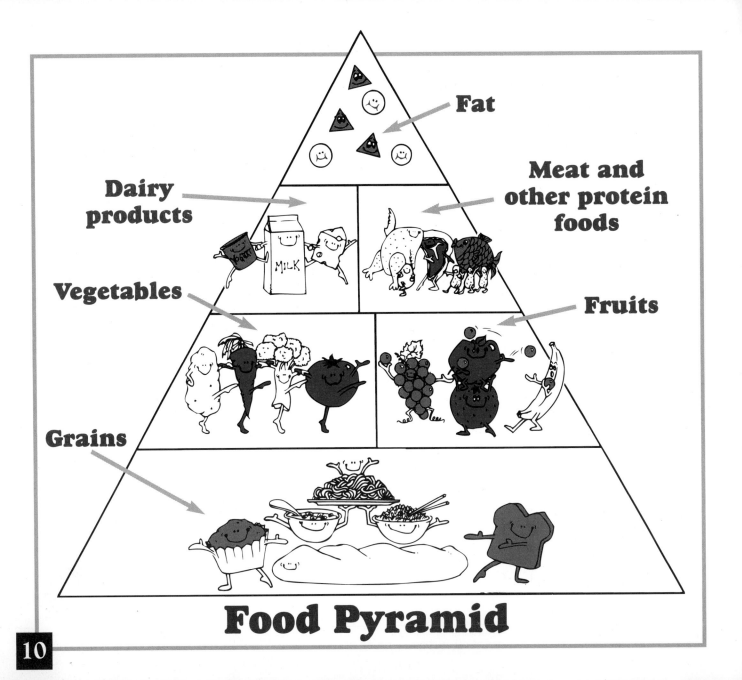

Food Pyramid

you are looking for protein. Lean meat, fish, and beans are excellent sources of protein.

Fat: You do need fat in your diet, just not too much! Treat yourself once in awhile with foods that have fat in them, just don't eat them all day, every day. Try to stay away from avocados, peanuts, and lots of butter. These are extremely high in fat!

The easiest way to eat for your heart is to eat a variety of different things. Your body would get sick and tired if you ate peanut butter and jelly for every meal! Some of the recipes in this book should be saved for special treats, and others are so healthful you can eat them frequently. In fact, you'll love them so much, you'll be able to tell those junk-food junkies to eat their hearts out!

Try these heart-healthy recipes!

Straight from Your Heart

Your heart has a big job to do, but somehow it always has time for a kind word or a special favor. Here are a few ideas to get your heart headed in the right direction!

Here is a list of things that you can do for other people. No matter how big or small you are, you can always treat someone else to a smile. This list is just to get you started — every day, see if you can find one thing to do that comes straight from your heart!

Read a book to a younger brother or sister

Hug your mom or dad

Clean up your room without being asked

Clear the table

Say thank you to your teacher

Share your cookies with a friend

Tell your brother or sister you're sorry

Write to your grandparents

Go run around outside with your dog
Save a nickel a week to give to someone else
Eat all the food on your plate
Say please when you want something
Make a valentine for someone — even when it's
    not Valentine's Day!

Bring your bus driver a warm
    muffin for breakfast
Ask if you can help
Make your own bed
Recycle
Don't argue
Smile!

These things may sound easy to do,
and you probably do some of them
every day already. See what else you
can do to make somebody else's day
a little brighter. Believe it or not
— your heart will feel terrific!

Heart-Smart Crossword Puzzle

Across

3. One of the three things needed to keep your heart running smoothly.

5. Your heart is as big as two clenched _____.

7. These blood vessels carry nutrients and oxygen to the body's cells.

Down

1. The oxygen-poor blood coming from the body is the color _____.

2. Oxygen-rich blood is _____.

4. Where your heart is located.

5. A diet which is low in _____ is best for your heart.

6. A bigger heart beats _____ than a smaller heart.

7. Clean _____ that is rich with oxygen helps keep your heart happy.

Word Games

A. How many words can you think of that rhyme with *heart*? See how many you can come up with and then challenge a friend to see who can come up with more!

B. How many different words can you make out of the title **HEARTS AND CRAFTS**? Use all of the letters in those three words to create new words but remember, if you see only one **H** you can use only one **H**! I'll get you started —

START

EAR

HAT

SAND

What's the record in your family?

Home-Cooked Hearts!

Here are some treats for you to make in the kitchen. The recipes labelled with this Healthy Heart symbol  are so good for your heart you can eat them often. The others should be saved for special occasions. Best of all, many of these foods look like hearts as well! The kitchen is a wonderful studio to create your hearts and crafts. Making good food is considered an art. Don't wait until Valentine's Day to decorate with hearts — jump into your "studio" and start enjoying them today!

Kitchen Tips

 Always work with clean hands, clean surfaces, and clean ingredients!

 Never use an electric kitchen machine without your grown-up helper!

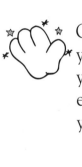 Check the recipe before you start to make sure you have everything you need!

 Clean up after you are done so that the kitchen is set for the next time you are ready to create!

 Measure everything carefully!

Valentine Party Planner

When it gets to be February, Valentine's Day is right around the corner and it's the perfect time to have a party! Grab your friends and make a date!

The first thing you will need is an **Invitation** to your party. Buy colored postcards at a stationary store. Use a rubber stamp of a heart and an inkpad to decorate the front of the card. Turn the card over and write the important information: what kind of party you are having, where it is, what time, what day, and your name. If you want your friends to call you to tell you if they are coming, put R.S.V.P. (the French abbreviation for "please respond!") and then your phone number. While you have your rubber stamp out, you might want to think of other things you can decorate — paper cups, tablecloth, lunch bags for holding valentines, and even place cards for the table.

Le Menu

- ♥ Cream of Tomato Soup with Crispy Heart Croutons
- ♥ Angel Food Cake with Chocolate and Strawberries
- ♥ Passion Punch

Valentine Party Games

One game you might play at your party is **Give the Host a Heart!** Get a big piece of paper (big enough for you to lie down on) and have a friend draw an outline around you. Add some details like eyes and ears, hair, fingernail polish, clothes, a baseball hat, sneakers, whatever you want! Next, cut out as many paper hearts as there are kids coming to your party.

When you are ready to play, provide markers or crayons so everyone can color and decorate his or her own heart. Put a rolled up piece of tape on the back of each heart. Hang your life-size picture on the wall, with eyes right at your eye level. Blindfold the person who is "up" and spin him around a few times gently. Aim your friend toward the picture and watch as he tries to stick the paper heart as close to where a real heart should go as possible. Everyone gets to do this. The one whose heart is closest to where it belongs wins!

Happy Hearts is another game to play. Cut large hearts out of construction paper and write each person's name on the front. Give everyone a heart and a marker or crayon and sit down in a circle. Now have everyone pass his or her heart to the right so that each has somebody else's heart. Write one nice thing about that person — does she have nice eyes? A pretty smile? A great dog? Tell funny jokes? Whatever you like about that person, write down! Pass the hearts to the right again and write one nice thing about the next person. Be sure to write only nice things! Keep doing this until your own heart gets back to you and then read what everyone has written.

Passion Punch

20 single-cup servings

• • WHAT YOU WILL NEED • • •

- Big punch bowl
- One 64-ounce bottle apple juice
- One 64-ounce bottle unsweetened cranberry juice
- One 6-ounce can apple juice concentrate, thawed
- One 1-liter bottle sparkling mineral water (for bubbles)
- Ice

Pour all of the above ingredients into the bowl and enjoy!

Cream of Tomato Soup

Approximately 4 to 5 servings

• • WHAT YOU WILL NEED • •

- 3½ cups chopped tomatoes
- 2 teaspoons sugar
- 2 tablespoons chopped onion
- 1 cup water
- 5 whole cloves
- 5 whole peppercorns
- ½ cup chopped fresh parsley
- 3 tablespoons margarine
- 3 tablespoons flour
- 3 cups skim milk
- ½ cup whole milk
- Salt and pepper
- Large saucepan
- Blender or food processor

1 In the large saucepan, combine the tomatoes, sugar, onion, and water. Add the cloves, peppercorns, and parsley. Ask your grown-up helper to bring the mixture to a simmer on the stove, then simmer on low, covered, for 25 minutes.

2 Ask your grown-up helper to put the tomato mixture in the blender or food processor and blend it until it is all smooth. Return the soup to the saucepan.

3 In another saucepan, melt the margarine. Blend in the flour. Gradually add the milks, and stir constantly until the mixture is thick and boiling. Add the boiling milk mixture to the tomato mixture. Serve hot with Crispy Heart Croutons on top!

Crispy Heart Croutons

Makes 12 to 16 croutons, enough for 4 or 5 bowls of soup

•••WHAT YOU WILL NEED•••

▶ 1 tablespoon margarine
▶ 4 slices of bread
▶ Garlic salt
▶ Frying pan
▶ Small heart-shaped cookie cutter
▶ Spatula

4. Use the spatula to flip the hearts. Sprinkle with garlic salt. Cook for 2 to 3 more minutes, or until the croutons are crispy and brown. Sprinkle on top of the tomato soup.

1. Use the cookie cutter to cut small hearts out of the bread. Try to get four hearts out of each slice.

2. Melt the margarine in the pan over medium heat.

3. Put the hearts in the pan, and stir *constantly* for 2 to 3 minutes.

Angel Food Cake with Chocolate and Strawberries

Serves 8 to 10

Angel Food Cake is a special treat — not only does it taste wonderful, but it's low in fat, too! Enjoy!

WHAT YOU WILL NEED

- 1 cup cake flour
- 1¼ cups sugar
- ½ teaspoon salt
- 10 egg whites
- 1 tablespoon water
- 1 tablespoon lemon juice
- 1 teaspoon cream of tartar
- ½ teaspoon vanilla extract
- ½ teaspoon almond extract
- Chocolate syrup
- Sliced strawberries
- Sifter
- 2 mixing bowls
- Whisk
- 9-inch tube pan

1 Preheat oven to 350°F. Sift the flour and ¼ cup of the sugar and the salt together into a bowl. Sift these ingredients two times.

2 In a separate bowl, use the whisk to whip the egg whites, water, and lemon juice. Add the cream of tartar. Whip the whites until they form little peaks when you pull the whisk up from them. Don't whip them too long — they should be stiff enough to stand, but not dry. (You can ask your helper to whip the egg whites with an electric mixer.)

3 Fold the vanilla and almond extracts into the egg whites. (Fold means to gently work vanilla into whites — don't stir too hard!)

4 Gradually whip in the remaining 1 cup sugar.

5 Sift the flour mixture into the egg whites, adding ¼ cup at a time, and gently folding in the flour after each addition, so that the egg whites do not get smooshed.

6 Pour the batter into the ungreased tube pan. Bake about 45 minutes.

 7 Let the cake cool upside down for at least 1 hour before removing from the pan.

 8 Using a cake divider, cut the angel food cake into slices.

9 Decorate the bottom of the cake plates with chocolate syrup, put the slice of cake on the chocolate, then place the sliced strawberries on top. Enjoy!

Carefully cut your strawberries in half from stem to tip. What do they look like? You guessed it . . . little, red hearts!

Heart-in-a-Basket

Serves 4

Start your day off right with a breakfast that highlights hearts!

·**WHAT YOU WILL NEED**··

- 4 eggs
- 4 pieces of bread
- 1–2 tablespoons margarine
- Heart-shaped cookie cutter
- Nonstick frying pan
- Spatula

1 Use your heart-shaped cookie cutter to cut a heart out of the center of each piece of bread. The hole in the bread will be the "basket" for your egg.

2 Put the margarine in the pan, and ask your helper to put the stove burner on medium.

3 When the margarine begins to bubble, carefully place one piece of bread **and** one cut-out heart side-by-side in the pan.

4 Quickly crack an egg, and drop it into the heart-shaped hole in the bread.

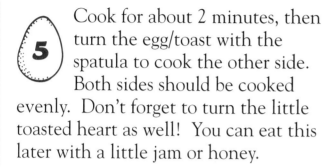 **5** Cook for about 2 minutes, then turn the egg/toast with the spatula to cook the other side. Both sides should be cooked evenly. Don't forget to turn the little toasted heart as well! You can eat this later with a little jam or honey.

6 Cook the egg until it is done the way you like it. After flipping, cook about 2 more minutes if you like your yolk runny, and 3 to 4 minutes if you like your yolk firm.

 7 Cook each piece of bread and egg the same way. Add more margarine to the pan if you need to.

 8 Put each of your Hearts-in-a-Basket on a plate. Serve with orange slices and juice.

Have a Heart for Our Bird Friends

Instead of grilling your little bread hearts, why not thread a string through the top and hang them on a tree outside for the birds!

Toasted Cheese Heart
Serves 1

Even lunch can be made extra special when you put your heart into it!
Try the "Hearts from around the World" — use low-fat cheese if you can —
and pretend you're sharing lunch with an international pal!

• • WHAT YOU WILL NEED • • •

- 2 slices of whole wheat bread for each sandwich
- Any type of cheese you like (Swiss, cheddar, Monterey jack, American)
- Sliced apple, sliced tomatoes, sprouts, salsa, mustard, herbs (optional)
- Large heart-shaped cookie cutter
- Spatula
- Aluminum foil

 1 Toast two slices of bread in a toaster until golden brown. Let cool.

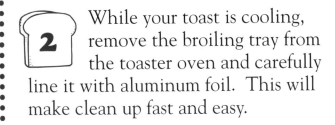 **2** While your toast is cooling, remove the broiling tray from the toaster oven and carefully line it with aluminum foil. This will make clean up fast and easy.

 3 Use your cookie cutter to carefully cut a heart out of the center of each slice of bread. Put a piece of cheese on top of each heart-shaped piece of toast.

4 Put the cheese-topped toast on the broiler tray and have your helper put the tray back in the toaster oven and turn the broiler on.

5 When the cheese is melted, have your helper turn the broiler off and remove the tray from the oven. Let the hearts cool for 2 or 3 minutes and then have your helper remove them from the tray with a spatula.

6 Close your sandwich up — cheese-side in, of course! Serve with a few carrot sticks or a pickle.

Hearts from around the World!

Mozzarella cheese, tomatoes, and basil make a Toasted Italian Heart!

Monterey jack cheese and salsa make a Toasted Mexican Heart!

Cheddar cheese, apple, and sprouts make a Toasted New England Heart!

Twice-Baked Potato
Serves 1

This is one of my favorite recipes from my mom. I guarantee you will like it — even more than French fries!
The amounts given in the ingredients list are enough for 1 potato.

• • • • • • • • • • WHAT YOU WILL NEED • • • • • • • • • • •

- 1 large baking potato
- 1 tablespoon low-fat sour cream
- 1 tablespoon plain nonfat yogurt
- 1 tablespoon chives
- Salt and pepper

- Knife
- Grated part-skim mozzarella cheese
- Pie plate
- Spoon
- Bowl
- Potato masher

 1 Preheat oven to 350°F.

 2 Place the potato in the pie plate, put it in the oven, and bake for 50 minutes. You will be able to squeeze it a little when it's done. Be careful — it will be very hot!

3 Have your helper cut an oval out of the top of the

potato, and then carefully dig out the baked potato with a spoon and place the insides in the bowl. Don't break the potato skin!

4 Use the potato masher to mix the sour cream, yogurt, chives, and salt and pepper into the potato in the bowl until it is creamy and smooth. To make it smoother, add a little skim or low-fat milk.

5 Using the spoon, put the mashed potato mixture back into the potato skin. Fill the skin right up to the top and sprinkle with mozzarella.

6 Put the potato back on the pie plate. Have your helper turn on the oven broiler. Broil the potato for 2 minutes, or until it's golden brown on top.

7 Twice-Baked Potatoes are good enough to make a whole meal! Just make some salad or cut up a carrot, and you've made dinner!

Painted Heart Bread

Here's an extremely simple — and healthy — way to let your artistic talent shine through in the kitchen! Grab your paint brush — a brand new brush or one that has only been used for food — and let's go!

• • WHAT YOU WILL NEED • •

- ½ cup milk
- 4 drops of red food coloring
- 2 slices of white bread for each sandwich
- Small bowl
- Brand new paint brush
- Toaster

1 Mix the milk and food coloring in the small bowl.

2 Set your slice of bread on the counter or work surface and use the paint brush and milk "paint" to paint a heart on your bread. Make one large heart or several little ones. Paint only one side of the bread, and be sure not to let the bread get too soggy!

3 When your picture is done, put the bread in the toaster on a **low** setting. The heat from the toaster will bake your heart into the bread.

4 Use the heart bread just as you would use any other bread. You can make a whole batch and store it in the 'fridge or in the freezer, so that you always have some on hand.

Let Your Imagination Go Wild

Paint smiley faces or sunshines for breakfast toast!

Paint numbers for a birthday party sandwich!

Paint stripes, dots, or squiggles, just for fun!

Heart-Shaped Raspberry Cake

Serves 12 to 16

• • WHAT YOU WILL NEED • • •

- ▶ 3 cups flour
- ▶ 2 cups sugar
- ▶ 4 teaspoons baking powder
- ▶ 1 teaspoon baking soda
- ▶ ½ teaspoon salt
- ▶ 2 cups low-fat sour cream
- ▶ 4 eggs, lightly beaten
- ▶ 2 cups raspberries
- ▶ ¼–½ cup confectioner's sugar
- ▶ One large and one small mixing bowl
- ▶ 8" x 8" non-stick square baking pan
- ▶ 8" non-stick round baking pan
- ▶ Large serving platter
- ▶ Extra raspberries for trim

1. Adjust your oven rack to be at the middle height, and preheat oven to 350°F.

2. In your large bowl, combine flour, sugar, baking powder, baking soda, and salt. In your small bowl, beat sour cream and eggs. Pour egg mixture into flour mixture and beat until smooth. Gently stir in the raspberries.

3. Pour half the batter into the square baking pan and the remaining half into the round pan.

4. Place both pans in the oven and bake for 20 minutes. When the cakes are finished cooking, allow them to cool completely in their pans.

5. Remove the cooled square cake from the pan and place it on your serving platter.

6. Remove the cooled round cake from the pan and place it on a clean cutting surface. Cut the round cake in half. Place the flat side of each round cake half on two meeting edges of the square cake to form a heart. You may need to move the square cake a little to give your heart room.

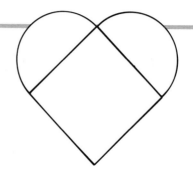

7. Just before serving, sprinkle the entire cake with confectioner's sugar. Be sure to cover the "seams" of your cake well so no one will figure out how you made it! Place extra raspberries to form a border.

Queen of Hearts Tart

Serves 8 to 10

Enjoy this while curled up with the wonderful story about the Queen of Hearts in Alice in Wonderland. Would you invite the Queen to join you for a slice? It's easy to make the crust for this tart in a food processor, if you have one. But always let a grown-up helper operate this machine. Your part is to measure all the ingredients carefully. If you don't have a food processor, use two forks or a pastry blender to mix the crust. You can freeze some of this, or eat it all for a special dessert or snack!

WHAT YOU WILL NEED

- 1 cup all-purpose flour
- 6 tablespoons margarine, cut into chunks
- 3 tablespoons confectioner's sugar
- ¼ cup margarine
- ½ cup sugar
- 2 eggs

- 1–2 teaspoons almond extract
- 1 pint fresh raspberries
- Food processor
- 10-inch tart pan
- Large bowl
- Electric mixer
- Wooden spoon

Preheat the oven to 350°F.

 Put the flour, 6 tablespoons of margarine, and confectioner's sugar into the food processor. Mix them together until they are crumbly. Pour the mixture into the tart pan, and use a spoon to press it against the bottom and sides to make the crust. Try to make the crust all the same thickness, with no thin or thick spots.

Put the ¼ cup margarine and the ½ cup sugar for the filling in a large bowl. Ask your helper to beat them with the electric mixer until they are fluffy. Add the eggs and almond extract and continue blending until everything is completely mixed together. Gently mix the filling with a wooden spoon until everything is combined.

Pour the filling into the crust. Put the pan in the oven and bake for 20 minutes, or until the crust is slightly browned.

Let it cool, then carefully cut it into 8 slices. Wash and drain the raspberries. Place them on top of your Queen of Hearts Tart to complete it!

Stained-Glass Heart Cookies

Yield varies, depending on size of cookies

You will love making and giving this beautiful dessert! You can arrange the cookies on a plate and serve them to your friends, or hang the cookies in the windows and let them catch the light.

• • WHAT YOU WILL NEED • •

- ½ cup margarine
- ½ cup sugar
- 1 egg
- 1¾ cups flour
- ½ teaspoon baking powder
- ½ teaspoon salt
- 1 teaspoon vanilla
- Red raspberry jam
- Large bowl
- Wooden spoon
- Plastic wrap
- Aluminum foil
- Cookie sheet

1 Mix the margarine in the bowl with your wooden spoon to soften it. Add the sugar and egg and beat until it is creamy. Add the remaining ingredients. Mix until the batter is smooth and stiff. You might need to take turns with your grown-up helper or a brother or sister — mixing dough is tiring work!

2 Cover the dough in the bowl with plastic wrap, and refrigerate for **at least** 2 hours.

3 Preheat the oven to 375°F. Place a piece of aluminum foil on the cookie sheet.

Take a small piece of the dough and roll it out into a rope that is about ¼ inch thick. Form your rope of dough into a heart shape — small or large, whatever you decide to create!

 Fill the inside of the heart with raspberry jam. Spread at least ¼ inch thick.

If you want to hang your hearts after you bake them, poke a toothpick hole in the dough at the very top of each heart before you put the cookies in the oven.

Bake the cookies for at least 10 minutes. The jam must bubble in order for it to harden as the cookies cool.

Let the cookies cool on the cookie sheet. Peel the aluminum foil off the back of each cookie.

Stone Soup: A Recipe

10 to 12 cups or 6 big bowls

*Read the wonderful story "Stone Soup" that follows
while you are waiting for your own pot of soup to boil!*

• • • WHAT YOU WILL NEED • • •

- 1 tablespoon olive oil
- 1 onion, chopped
- 2 carrots, peeled and chopped
- 2 potatoes, diced into small pieces
- 1 cup chopped green beans
- 3 celery stalks, chopped
- 1 cup chopped tomatoes

- Water (about 5 cups)
- 3 low-salt chicken or vegetable bouillon cubes
- 1 large clean stone for taste
- 1 cup rotelle pasta
- Salt and pepper
- Parmesan cheese
- Large soup pot

 Heat the oil in the large pot and sauté the onion in it over medium heat for about 4 to 5 minutes or until soft.

Add the rest of the chopped vegetables to the pot, and stir so that all are mixed in and covered with oil. Cook for 5 minutes.

 Add the pasta, and cook for 10 more minutes. Sprinkle with the salt and pepper. Serve in a bowl with a sprinkle of Parmesan cheese.

Add enough water to the pot to cover the vegetables. Add the stone and bouillon cubes. Put the lid on, and let the soup simmer for 30 minutes.

Chopping Vegetables

◆ Wash all of the vegetables with a scrub brush before chopping!

◆ Help your grown-up helper by peeling the carrots!

◆ Never use a knife without your grown-up helper! If your helper lets you chop, be sure to keep your fingers away from the knife blade, and pay close attention to what you are doing!

Stone Soup: A Folk Tale

Retold by Jennifer Storey Gillis

There once was a small group of peaceful soldiers who were coming home from war. They were very tired and hungry, and as they passed through a small village, they knocked on a door to see if they could get something to eat. The people of the village had been warned that the soldiers were coming, and being afraid and very poor, the villagers decided to keep everything they had for themselves. As the soldiers knocked on each door of the village, they were told that there was nothing to eat.

The soldiers gathered in the town square to decide what to do. They needed food and shelter, but it was obvious that the people of the village were not going to cooperate. "It's time to make Stone Soup," said one soldier to the rest, in a voice loud enough for the peeking townspeople to hear. And so the soldiers set off to gather the ingredients.

The first soldier went knocking and asked for a pot in which to make the Stone Soup.

"How can you make soup from a stone?" asked an old woman.

"It's a magic soup that promises plenty for all," replied the soldier. And so she lent him her big, black pot and some

water to get him started.

The second soldier went knocking and asked for a stone.

"How can you make soup from a stone?" asked the man who came to the door.

"It's a magic soup that promises plenty for all," replied the soldier. And so the man gave him a stone and some carrots he had, for taste.

The third soldier had started a fire in the town square and was busy stirring the water and the stone in the big, black pot. The soldiers looked so happy and eager for their soup that the townspeople became very interested and started to bring out bits and pieces of food that they found around the house, just "to add some taste" to the Stone

Soup. Different people brought out different things — a few potatoes, a handful of green beans, a stalk or two of celery, a tomato, an onion, even a fish just caught in the stream that ran through the town. Nobody had enough to make a whole pot of soup themselves, but everyone had a little bit to add. Each person threw his or her contribution into the pot, mumbling all the while that, "you can't make soup from a stone!" But the soldiers were optimistic, and it made the townspeople eager for the soup as well.

After a short time the soldiers told the people to run and get their bowls. They did as they were told and came back to taste the Stone Soup. It was delicious! There was plenty for everyone, and they ate and talked and danced into the night. Everyone was happy and full as they hadn't been in years. All this soup . . . all from a stone!

Heart Art!

Whether you are creating in the kitchen with a wooden spoon or in the family room with a paint brush, adding a few hearts seems to make every project more fun! The next few pages will give you ideas for creating games and gifts — all with hearts. All you need are some basic materials, a helper, and your creativity and imagination. For best results — put your heart into it!

Heart-Shaped Clay Checkers

Making crafts with real clay is so much fun!
Put on a smock, roll up your sleeves, and dig in!

·· WHAT YOU WILL NEED ·· ·

- 2–3 sticks of self-hardening clay
- Rolling pin
- Small heart-shaped cookie cutter
- Standard checker board
- Opaque paint (two colors) and paint brush

 Roll the clay out on a clean, smooth surface. It should be about ½ inch thick.

 Using the cookie cutter, cut out twenty-four hearts.

Carefully pick them up and put them on a flat surface to dry where they can stay for at least three days without being disturbed.

 After three days, check your checkers. If you can't squeeze them out of shape when you pinch them slightly, they are hard enough to use. If they aren't quite ready, be patient and let them sit for another day. Next, paint half of them one color and half in a second color. Let them dry again.

 When they are ready, set the twelve checkers of each color up on your checker board, get yourself a partner, and you are ready to play.

Tips for Working with Clay

◆ Put something underneath the clay when you are working with it. A plastic drop cloth is easy to work on, and it's reusable as well.

◆ Be patient while the clay is drying. Make sure your project is thoroughly dry before playing with it.

◆ Paint your checkers in great colors to give your game an extra ZING!

Heart Pots

Here's another clay project to enjoy. A heart-shaped pot would make a perfect gift for someone you love — or perhaps you could store your Heart-Shaped Clay Checkers in it.

•••WHAT YOU WILL NEED•••

- Self-hardening clay
- Medium-size heart-shaped cookie cutter
- Spatula
- Flexible fingers!

1 Find a clean, smooth surface to work on.

2 Using your rolling pin, roll out a small piece of the clay. It should be about ½ inch thick and big enough to fit your cookie cutter.

3 Cut a heart out of the clay and remove the scraps from around it. This heart is going to be the bottom of your pot! Work the scraps back into the rest of the clay with your fingers.

4 Roll a lemon-size piece of clay into a smooth ball. Put the ball on the table and using your **hands** as a rolling pin, roll the clay into a long thin snake. The snake should be as thick as your thumb when you are done.

5 Carefully start wrapping the snake around the edge of the heart shape you cut in step 3.

Little by little, build up the sides of the pot by laying the snake on top of the previous row as you go around the heart shape. Stop whenever you think it is tall enough — or when you run out of clay!

6 Gently push the coils of clay together so that there are no cracks in the walls. Make sure that the coils are firmly pushed onto the heart-shaped bottom, so that when it dries, it will not fall apart.

7 Using the spatula, carefully move the pot to a warm dry spot where it can dry completely. After three or four days of drying, your pot should be ready to hold your little treasures!

Salt-Dough Heart Jewelry

This is a very simple way to wear your heart on your sleeve —
or around your neck or your wrist!
You can paint your jewelry or leave it natural.

•••WHAT YOU WILL NEED•••

- 2 cups whole-wheat flour
- 1 cup salt
- ¾ cup water
- Mixing bowl
- Cookie sheet
- Nonstick cooking spray
- Rolling pin
- Heart-shaped cookie cutter
- Spatula
- Toothpick
- Timer
- Heavy-duty white thread
- Watercolors and paint brush (optional)
- Dish towel

1 Combine the flour, salt, and water in the bowl, and mix with your hands until it forms an elastic dough that is easy to knead with your hands. This may take some experimenting — if it is too dry, add a little more water; if it is too wet and sticky, add a bit more flour.

2 Coat the cookie sheet with nonstick spray.

3 Roll a small piece of dough into a ball. Put it on the table and use a rolling pin to roll it out until it is about ¼ inch thick.

Using your cookie cutter, cut out as many hearts as you can. Use the spatula to move the hearts to the cookie pan. With the toothpick, poke a small hole in the center of each heart.

To make small round beads, take small pieces of dough and rub them into little balls with your hands. Place these on the cookie sheet, and put a hole through the middle of each one.

Preheat your oven to 170°F. Ask your grown-up helper to put the cookie sheet in the oven. Set a timer for 1 hour.

After the hour is up, carefully check the hearts. If they are hard when you tap them, they are done. If you can indent them with your finger, put them in for another 15 minutes. Pieces thicker than ¼ inch thick usually take longer than 1 hour to "cook." Don't burn yourself when you test the clay! Let them cool for at least ½ hour before using them.

Dough Tips

♥ While you are working with one piece of dough, cover the rest with a dish towel so that it does not dry out.

♥ To color the dough, add a few drops of food coloring to the water as you mix it.

♥ You can not microwave this recipe!

To Paint!

◆ Give all the hearts a white base coat. Other colors painted over it will be brighter.

◆ Paint hearts all the colors of the rainbow — not just pink or red!

◆ Let them dry completely before stringing.

To String!

◆ Cut a piece of white thread that will fit around your neck or wrist **loosely.**

◆ String one bead and tie a big knot in the end of it. Continue stringing beads side by side. When you get a third of the way done, start using one heart, then one bead, one heart, one bead, and so on until the string is two-thirds of the way filled. Finish with just beads.

When you are finished, have your helper tie the two ends of the string together in a tight knot. Make your necklace large enough so that you can take your necklace off your head without untying it.

To Make a Pin!

◆ Don't make a hole through this heart before baking it.

◆ Take your painted heart, and turn it over so that it is lying face down on the table.

◆ Using some strong glue or masking tape, fix a safety pin to the back of the heart. It should open and close easily.

◆ Let the glue dry, then wear it on your favorite sweater or shirt.

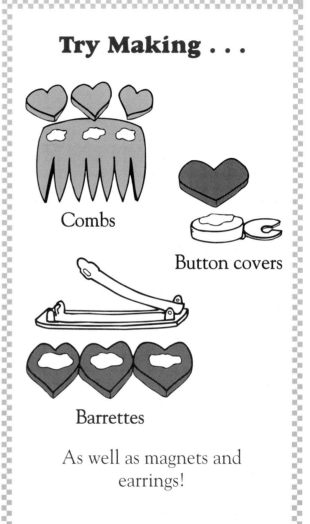

Try Making . . .

Combs

Button covers

Barrettes

As well as magnets and earrings!

Heart Stencils

Have your grown-up helper work at your side, and you can create terrific T-shirts. Try putting a heart on the end of your white cotton sneakers or your recyclable lunch bag! You can buy fabric paint and stencil brushes at craft stores.

·· **WHAT YOU WILL NEED** ·· ·

- ▶ Washable fabric paint
- ▶ Stencil paint brush
- ▶ Plain T-shirt
- ▶ Stencil sheet
- ▶ Masking tape
- ▶ Old newspaper
- ▶ Pencil

1 Make sure your T-shirt is washed and dried before you start stenciling.

2 Put the newspaper inside the shirt so that the paint does not absorb into the back of the shirt while you are working.

3 Place the T-shirt on a smooth surface and get a helper to hold it in place for you!

4 Tape the stencil right where you want it on the shirt. Make sure it is straight and in the middle.

5 Carefully begin dabbing paint on the stencil to print the heart on the shirt. Use only a small amount of paint on your brush and work slowly so that the paint goes only where you want it to. When you are finished, take the stencil sheet off the shirt.

6 Follow the directions with the paint for setting the design. This usually means your helper must iron the shirt before you wear or wash it.

7 Clean up the paint and the newspapers, and put on your brand new heart T-shirt!

How to Make a Stencil Sheet

Take a piece of oak tag or a manilla file folder, and with a pencil, trace the shape you want to stencil. If you want one big heart, trace around a big cookie cutter. If you want three small hearts in a row, trace around a small cookie cutter three times. (Or use the patterns on page 58.) This is the fun part — you can make any design you would like!

Poke a hole in the center of the design that you have traced, and carefully cut out the shape. Now you are ready to stencil!

55

Heart Jigsaw Puzzle

This puzzle is fun and easy to make. Store the puzzle in an envelope for another day. You can even send it to a friend!

⋅ ⋅ WHAT YOU WILL NEED ⋅ ⋅

- ▶ Marking pens or crayons
- ▶ A piece of cardboard
- ▶ Scissors
- ▶ Big envelope with clasp

1. Using the crayons or markers, draw and color a heart picture. Make sure you fill up the whole piece of cardboard. Can you think of a way to make a message in your picture?

2. With scissors, carefully cut the cardboard picture into about ten pieces. The pieces should be unusual and curvy shapes, but make sure they are not too small!

3. Now comes the hard part — match up the lines, colors, and edges, and put your puzzle back together!

4. Put the puzzle away in the envelope and save it for another day.

Valentines!

With pretty valentines like these, you'll wish that February 14th came around more than once a year! There are all sorts of ways to make a valentine. These are just a few of the basic ideas. Take them and create your own designs!

··· WHAT YOU WILL NEED ···

- Red, pink, white, and purple construction paper
- Scissors
- Craft glue
- Markers or crayons
- Paper doilies

Valentine Card #1

1. Take an 8½" x 11" piece of purple construction paper and fold it in half.

2. Take a 5½" x 11" piece of red construction paper and fold it in half. Use the "Half-a-Heart Cutting

Technique" on the next page to cut a heart out of the red paper.

3. From pink construction paper, cut out another heart a little bit smaller than the red heart.

4. Glue the red heart in the middle of the folded purple card, then glue the pink heart on top of the red heart.

Bleeding-hearts are flowers that bloom again year after year, with soft, feathery leaves, arched stems, and rose-red, heart-shaped flowers!

Half-a-Heart Cutting Technique

Use the outline shown here to create your own heart patterns.

1 Trace or photocopy the patterns. Cut them out.

2 Take a piece of construction paper and fold it in half.

3 Place the straight side of each size heart pattern on the fold of the paper. Draw around the patterns.

4 Cut along the lines. Be sure not to cut the fold!

5 Unfold the paper — you will have four different sized hearts!

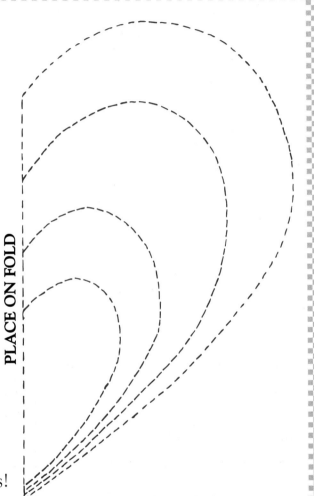

PLACE ON FOLD

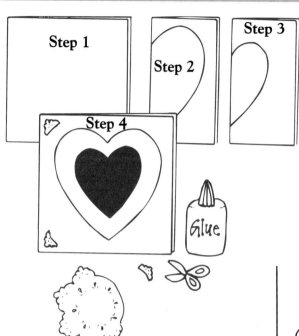

Step 1

Step 2

Step 3

Step 4

Glue

Valentine Card #2

This card uses a circular doily as the base for your designs.

1. Cut out a large red heart that will fit in the center of the doily. Glue it on and let it dry.

2. Make much smaller hearts out of pink and purple construction paper

5. Using the lace-like doily, trim around the outside of the red heart. Use just a little glue and small pieces of doily to make a 3-D effect. Let the glue dry.

6. Write your message on the inside of the purple card.

and glue these all over the large red heart. Let all these dry.

3. Use the markers or crayons to write your messages inside the little hearts.

Valentine Card #3

This is a surprise valentine card. It doesn't look like a heart until you open it all the way up and then . . . wow!

1. Make a large red heart and fold it in half down the middle.

2. Cut small hearts from other colored construction paper.

3. Glue them to the inside of the large heart. Decorate around them with markers or crayons. Add your message.

Why Valentine's Day?

There were two Valentines, St. Valentine of Rome and St. Valentine of Termi. Each had his feast day on February 14.
    In the late Middle Ages, people began sending love notes on this day, because it was thought that February 14 began the mating season for birds! Love was in the air!

Step 1
Step 2
Roses are Red Violets are blue I'm so glad To have a friend like you!
Step 3